T0128435

In God We Trust

B. B. Hicks

WESTBOW
P R E S S®
A DIVISION OF THOMAS NELSON
& ZONDERVAN

Scripture quotations are taken from the
King James Version of the Bible.

WestBow Press books may be ordered through
booksellers or by contacting:

WestBow Press
A Division of Thomas Nelson & Zondervan
1663 Liberty Drive
Bloomington, IN 47403
www.westbowpress.com
1 (866) 928-1240

ISBN: 978-1-9736-5683-8 (sc)
ISBN: 978-1-9736-5684-5 (e)

Library of Congress Control Number: 2019902871

Print information available on the last page.

WestBow Press rev. date: 03/29/2019

"I will say of the Lord, He is my refuge and
my fortress: my God; in Him will I trust."
Psalms 91:2 (KJV)

Contents

Introduction

"In God We Trust" is the official motto for the United States of America and can be found written many different places in our country. It is found, for instance, on our national currency, on many car tags, bumper stickers, signs, and posters. The list can go on and on, as to where this motto can be found written, but my question is: Do we really trust in God? Have we, as a nation, left our first love? Have we become a godless nation or a nation of many gods? Have we become silent Christians, letting anything go, or are we just going through the motions or going along just to get along – not making waves or taking a stand on anything, whether right or wrong? Have we become lukewarm in our Christian walk, or have we lost our zeal? Are we catering to itching ears that only want to hear a portion of the gospel? Have we stopped telling the whole truth of the Word of God, the part that tells us about consequences of our actions and how one day we will all have to stand before a righteous God and give an account for our every idle word and deed? (Matthew 12:36). The theme of many Christian messages today focuses on the goodness of God and how He is a loving and kind God who wants us to grow and prosper. This is all true, but God is also a just and righteous God, and He is not a respecter of person. He will execute judgment on that great day of wrath (Romans 14:10; 2 Peter 2:9).

This book is a clarion call to the nation, as well as to the church; to turn back to God. We, as people of God, need to put first things first and God should be first in our lives. We should perform a self-assessment to determine what are our priorities and what is first on our agenda. The Bible tells us that God is a jealous God and He wants to be first in all things (Exodus 20:4-5).

Are we now facing insurmountable problems because we have taken God out of our homes, schools, churches, and now our nation? Have we taken God out of our lives? Have we become too busy for God? Are we so preoccupied with the cares of this world or the things of this world that we don't take time or make time for our God? The Bible tells us that if we, God's people who are called by His name, will humble ourselves and pray, seek His face, and turn from our wicked ways, then God will hear from heaven and will forgive our sins and will heal our land (2 Chronicles 7: 14). If you have watched television, read an internet or news article, or if you are up-to-date on current events, then you should already know that our land needs healing.

We need Jesus - both you and I need Jesus. The whole world need Jesus. We all need salvation. The Word of God lets us know that "all have sinned and come short of the glory of God" (Romans 3:23). God offers the whole world salvation through His Son Jesus. Salvation itself signifies that we are asking Jesus Christ to be our Lord and Savior and that we want Him to be the head of our lives. When we get saved or born again, this means that we hear and believe the gospel. We are to "confess with our mouth the Lord Jesus Christ and believe in our heart that God has raised Jesus from the dead" (Romans 10:9). We should then invite Jesus to come into our hearts and be our Lord and Savior. When we do this, we are asking for God to save us from our sins and for Him to lead and guide us. When we give our lives to Jesus Christ, we become new creatures in Christ and our priorities should change. God's will should become our will. We should not only want God to save us from eternal damnation, but for Him to guide us, keep us, and for His will to be done in our lives. Therefore, when we profess to be Christians, God and His will should be first on our agenda.

So, I ask again, what are our priorities and what is first on our agenda? On who or what are we trusting? Are we putting our trust in our finances, ourselves, other people, or things rather than in the almighty God? We are to put our trust in God because He is worthy of our trust. We can safely trust Him to help us, save us, and deliver us, because He will never let us down. God is trustworthy. We can put our confidence in God because we need Him, and without Him we can do nothing (John 15:5). As believers in Christ, we are to put our trust in the Lord. As we grow in Christ, we should become so completely committed to Him and His Word that we mature as Christians. Maturity in Christ means we are anchored in the Lord and His Word, and as mature saints, we should already know that we can trust God and depend on Him. When we get to know God for who He really is and what He stands for, we will see His enormous power and the grace and mercy He has for His people. We will find out that what is impossible with man is always possible with God. Trusting God is easy when our backs are up against the wall and we don't have any other way out, but what about trusting God in the good times, when nothing is going on, when things are going well? We can trust God in the good times and during the bad times. Some people put more confidence in their car, job, or some other inanimate object than in their God.

God is all powerful, all knowing, and He is everywhere; besides Him there is no other God. God is the beginning and the end, the great I AM, the true, living, and only wise God (Revelation 1:8; Exodus 3:14; 1 Timothy 1:7; Jude 1:25). There is nothing too hard for God – no problem, sickness, trouble, distress, or any other situation. God can do whatever His Word says He can do. When we get to know God, and develop a personal relationship with Him, we will discover this for ourselves and it will become easy for us to trust God. As we grow in Christ, we will learn that we can trust God and depend on Him to take care of all our needs. We are to always put our trust in God, because He can do exceeding abundantly above all we ask or think (Ephesians 3:20). God has never failed, and He causes us to always triumph in Christ Jesus (2 Corinthians 2:14).

Some of you may be wondering: what does it mean to have faith in God, or how can I trust God when my situation is so bleak/hopeless, or how do I know when I'm truly trusting God? Maybe you are in a backslidden condition and don't know how to come back to God.

Perhaps you have never made Jesus Christ your Lord and Savior and would like to get to know Him. It is never too late to get to know God, no matter what type of life you have lived, or how old you are, because you are never too old to get to know Jesus Christ. Therefore, you should never believe Satan's lies if he tells you that it is too late to come to Christ, or you are too old, or since you have lived a lifetime in sin, that God will never forgive you or use you for the building of His kingdom. These are all lies of the enemy, because as long as there is breath still in your body, you can come to God and He will in no wise turn you away or reject you (John 6:37). God loves all of us and wants the best for us. God will welcome us with open arms. God has been there waiting for us all the time. Matthew 7:7 tells us to "ask, and it shall be given you; seek and ye shall find; knock, and it shall be open unto you." The Holy Bible also let us know that God doesn't want for any of His children to perish (2 Peter 3:9).

This is a wake-up call to the church as well as to our nation to turn back to God. This is a call for the lost, the saints, all nations, and for all people everywhere to get to know God or to turn back to God and to the former things of old. It is a call for us to earnestly put our trust in the Lord and put Him first in our lives. Are you trusting God? Do you believe in God and His Word? Are you a hearer and doer of the Word? Are you living according to the will of God? Are you telling others about the goodness of Jesus Christ? Are you taking a stand for what is right and for the truth that is based on the Word of God? Is God first on your agenda? Do you know Jesus Christ as your Lord and Savior?

Are you currently attending a Bible-believing, Bible-teaching church? Have you compromised on the Word of God or on your own moral or Christian beliefs? I ask these questions to raise your awareness and bring to your attention the current condition of our church, our nation, and for us to take a closer look at ourselves. I do not mean to imply or say that all churches or all pastors need a wake-up call, because this is truly not the case for there are many churches and many pastors (including my own) who are doing the will of God. However, this is a call for our nation, and for the churches and pastors who have compromised on the Word of God, to return to God.

This book is also for those who are lost and don't know Jesus as their Lord and Savior. This is a cry for them to come to the only true and living God, and this is my attempt to show them the way or pathway to God. This pathway is only found and accessible through God's Son, Jesus Christ. In this book, I will review a few Scriptures taken from the Holy Bible that will show who God is, what He stands for, and why we can always safely put our trust in Him. Because God is faithful, worthy of our trust, and is a good, just and righteous God. As you read the pages of this book, look to God and His Word for a better understanding on how to:

1. Get to know God
2. Trust God
3. Turn back to God
4. Stay connected to God

Chapter 1

Getting to Know God

Man will never fully understand all the mysteries of God and all of His wonderful works and power, but by reading the Word of God we can get a better understanding of who God is and what He is all about. When trying to gain a better understanding of God and develop a closer relationship with Him, it is important for us to study the Word of God. James 4:8 tells us that when we draw near to God, He draws near to us. The Bible also tells us that God's thoughts and ways are much higher than ours and that God is not like man that He should lie because God will always do what His Word says He will do (Isaiah 55:8-9; Numbers 23:19). God is who His Word says He is. He is a God defined as love (1 John 4:8).

The Holy Scriptures tells us that God is the creator of the heaven and the earth and of all the inhabitants that dwell therein (Genesis 1:1). In the beginning, God said let there be and there was (Genesis 1:3). God created everything that was created (John 1:3).

God's power is unlimited and surpasses all the laws of the earth. God is a spirit, a supernatural being: He is the "Alpha and Omega the beginning and the ending" (Revelation 1:8). God is outside of time, as we know time, because "one day is with the Lord as a thousand years, and a thousand years as one day" (2 Peter 3:8). God is the "Great I AM" which means that He is everything we need Him to be (Exodus 3:13-14).

God can do the impossible (Luke 18:27) and He is a miracle worker. We often times will see God work miracles in our lives when there is nothing humanly possible for us to do to fix our own problem. This is because, it is during these times, when we are feeling hopeless, that we will then turn to God or put our trust in God for our solution. We would see even more miracles if we would trust God more often, or if we relied on Him, instead of our own self efforts. God is the only one who can help us or save us during times of impossible situations. "God is our refuge and strength, a very present help in the times of trouble" (Psalm 46:1).

We can also learn more about God through our own personal experience with Him. Our individual encounters with God will provide some information to us about the nature of God. The Word of God shows how many individuals in the Bible learned of God through their own personal interaction with Him. They were transformed by their encounter with God. The character of God was manifested or was made known to these individuals who had encounters with Him. They left their interactions with God with a better understanding of God; having gained additional knowledge about the character, and power of God that was not previously known to them before their interactions with Him.

Moses, Abraham, Isaac, Jacob, the woman at the

well, Hagar, and Saul/Paul are just a few who had such an encounter with God. They left their encounters able to see new characteristics of God that was not previously known to them before their interaction. I will list a few of their revelations that I notice in Scripture, but this list is not meant to be all-inclusive of the all people who had interactions with God, nor for the knowledge that was revealed to them, from their encounter with God.

Moses: He learned that God can speak from a burning bush, that God is a miracle worker, and a deliverer. Additionally, he learned that God can part the Red Sea, and subdue your enemies so that you will "see them again no more forever" (Exodus 3:1-7, 7:10, 20, 8:5, 17, 21, 9:2, 8, 14, 18, 10:4, 21, 11:4-7, 13:21, 14:15-16,).

Abraham: He learned from his encounters with God, that God can do the impossible, that God keeps His promises, and that God is a provider (Genesis 17:1-1-8, 17-21, 18:9-14, 21:1-3, 22:1-14).

Isaac: He learned that obedience to God can lead to a hundredfold blessing (Gen 26:1-3, 12).

Jacob: He learned that being persistent with God, will pay off and that when God changes your name, He also changes your destiny (Genesis 32:24-30).

The woman at the well: She learned that God knows everything and that you can't hide anything from God. She also discovered that the promised Messias had come (John 4:3-43).

Hagar: She learned that the God of Abraham was a God who sees her and she learned that God will help you in times of trouble (Genesis 16:13, 21:14-19).

Saul (Paul): He learned that God can give your life new meaning and new purpose, and that God gives assignments to obey, Saul (Paul) also learned that God can change your name and your mind, and that God can use you for His glory and for the building of His Kingdom despite your past actions (the book of Acts, Romans, 1 & 2 Corinthians, Galatians, Ephesians, Philippians, Colossians, 1 & 2 Thessalonians, 1&2 Timothy, Titus, and Philemon; all in their entirety).

In getting to know God, it is paramount that we develop a personal relationship with Him.

When we accept Jesus Christ into our lives, we are no longer the same person, we become new creatures in Christ (2 Corinthians 5:17). When we read the Word, go to God in prayer, spend quality time with God, and assemble ourselves together with other believers at the Lord's house, it gives us opportunities to learn more of God and grow closer to God.

Have you accepted Jesus as your Lord and Savior? Does your life have meaning? When we accept Jesus, God transforms our lives and this transformation will change our outlook on life. Knowing God and His Word helps us gain insight into ourselves and our lives.

God gives our lives purpose and meaning that will also help us understand the events that are taking place in the world today. Have you ever wondered why you were born or what is your purpose in life? We were all born for a purpose, but it is up to us to fulfill God's plan for our lives. God created mankind with purpose in mind. Have you ever had an encounter with God? If so, did you leave your encounter a different person, like Saul, who was changed after he met Jesus Christ on the road to Damascus? (Acts 9). Saul was totally changed after his encounter with God and he later went on to become Paul the apostle who accomplished many great works for the Lord. Have you ever been in trouble, in distress, or sick with an unfavorable health prognosis? Have you ever been in a bad situation with no way out and you didn't know what to do? God is the answer for our every problem or situation that is going on in our lives. God is the solution. God is a problem solver, a heart fixer, and a mind regulator.

God is our creator, a way maker, a lawyer in the court room, and a doctor in the sick room. God is an all-knowing God and He knows what to do, even when we don't know what to do. When we are born again we are partnered with the almighty God and "if God be for us, who can be against us?" (Ephesians 4:30; Romans 8:31). As saints, we are on the winning team and everything will work out for our good! (Romans 8:28). God causes us to always win in Christ (2 Corinthians 2:14). Satan is already a defeated adversary and no weapon formed against us will prosper (Isaiah 54:17). God can do anything but fail because God is sovereign, all powerful, is everywhere, and He is Lord who sits on His throne in heaven. When we accept Jesus Christ in our lives we are no longer the same. It is God that makes all the difference in our lives. He gives hope where there is no hope and gives us joy, peace, and love. He equips us with everything we need to live a successful Christian life

(Philippians 4:7; Isaiah 26:3; Romans 8:34; Matthew 6:33). All we have to do is call on the name of Jesus and ask Him for whatever we need (John 14:13-14). Jesus Christ said in John 16:23 that "Whatsoever ye shall ask the Father in my name, He will give it you." Matthew 6:8 tells us that God already knows what we need before we ask Him, but He still wants us to ask Him and to ask Him in faith, believing and not doubting. God has everything we need, and He is always with us and because of who God is, we can always and confidently put our trust in the Lord. Because God is faithful, worthy, just, good and a righteous God who is full of grace, mercy and truth (Psalm 7:9; Ezra 9:15; Deuteronomy 32:4). The Word tells us that God's mercy is renewed every morning (Lamentations 3:22-23). God will never leave us nor forsake us (Hebrews 13:5). His faithfulness is shown repeatedly by His consistency; He never changes, He never lies, He never fails, He is always there when we need Him (Malachi 3:6; Zephaniah 3:5; Isaiah 55:11; Matthew 28:20).

God is worthy of our trust because He is reliable, and dependable. He is our refuge in the time of trouble, and we can depend on Him because He will never let us down (Deuteronomy 7:9; Psalm 9:9; 2 Timothy 3:3).

God loves us and wants the best for us (John 3:16). God has such a love for mankind that He sent His only begotten Son to die for us. It is because of God's great love for us that the question was raised in the Holy Scriptures: "What is man that thou are mindful of him?" (Psalm 8:4-6). It is because of God's love for us that He gives us the opportunity to repent and come to Jesus Christ before judgment. Because Judgment

Day is coming, and no one will be exempt, neither the rich, nor the poor, the young nor old because God is not a respecter of person and what goes for one goes for all (Acts 10:34). The Bible tells us that God doesn't want anyone to perish (2 Peter 3:9). We will all have the choice to either accept or reject Jesus Christ as our Lord and Savior but the decisions we make will have lasting consequences for us. Our decisions will determine whether we live or die. When we choose Jesus Christ as our Lord and Savior, we are choosing eternal life but if we reject Christ, we are choosing death, hell and destruction. Choose Jesus and live!

We don't want to suffer the consequences for making bad decisions for our lives because when we reject Jesus Christ as our Lord and Savior, we are bound for eternal damnation and everlasting separation from a loving God. But take heart, because it is not too late to choose Jesus and live!

There are many people who already have heard about God. Some have known about God since early childhood, but for whatever reason they have rejected the gospel, or never believed or accepted Jesus Christ as their Lord and Savior. However, when trouble arises in their lives, many will then turn to God or return to God. But why not come to Jesus Christ right now, before trouble comes, before it is too late? Come to Jesus while you can, while the blood is still running warm in your veins. Because tomorrow is not promised and may very well be too late. The Bible tells us that mankind will be without excuse if they reject Jesus Christ because we all have been created with the innate ability to know there is a God, and His existence can be clearly seen and understood through the observation of the things seen in creation (Romans 1:18-21). Therefore, we should choose Jesus and live!

Reading God's Word on a regular basis is an excellent way to learn more of God. When we read the Word of God, it helps us to understand who God is and see how much He loves us. Hearing God's Word will cause our faith to grow because "faith cometh by hearing and hearing by the Word of God" (Romans 10:17). We can also learn more about God when someone tells us about Jesus Christ: this is when they share the gospel of the kingdom of God and tell us the good news of Jesus Christ. When we are exposed to the gospel or good news of Jesus Christ, we will hear of God and of His Son, Jesus Christ. It is through the Word of God that we will learn about God the Father, God the Son, and God the Holy Spirit. It is through God's Word that we learn about the Son of God, Jesus Christ, and about all He has done for us. The Holy Scriptures tell us that God so loved the world that He gave His only begotten Son, Jesus Christ, who came down from heaven to earth to be born of a virgin, to save the world from their sins; so that whosoever believe in Him should not perish but have everlasting life. (John 3:16; Luke 1:26-27; Romans 6:23).

The Word also lets us know that Jesus Christ, who knew no sins, became sin for us, so that we might become the righteousness of God (2 Corinthians 5:21). Jesus bled and died on the cross so that we might live (2 Corinthians 5:15, 21; 1 Peter 2:24). Jesus Christ paid the ultimate price for our sin by freely giving up His life for us (1 Peter 2:24). The good news doesn't end there;

Jesus Christ defeated death and Satan and on the third day He arose from the dead with all power in His hand, and at the appointed time, He ascended back to heaven, where He is now seated on the right hand of God, His Father, making intercession for us (Matthew 28:18; Acts 1:9-11; Romans 8:34). After we hear this gospel, we must believe what we have heard; this is faith, trusting in God and believing His Word.

Because of what Jesus Christ did for us, salvation is available and free to all who believe in Him. Salvation is a gift from God (Ephesians 2:8-9). This Scripture tells us that it is by grace that we are saved through faith and not of ourselves; it is a gift of God. This passage of Scripture also let us know that salvation is not achieved through works lest any man should boast (Ephesians 2:9). Therefore, if you don't know Jesus Christ as your Lord and Savior and you want to get to know Him, you can, because the gift of salvation is free and available to anyone who will believe. This free gift is available to us because of what Jesus Christ did for us on the cross. He freely gave His life so that we might live. Jesus Christ has already done the work; He already paid the price for our sins and for our salvation with His own blood. All we have to do is believe and receive this blessing from the Lord.

After hearing, believing, and accepting Jesus Christ as Lord and Savior, we are born again. If you don't know the Lord, please take this opportunity right now to come to Him and get to know Him. Do it today while you can because tomorrow is not promised. We should take advantage of this gift that God has so freely offered because salvation is available and accessible to all of us.

The only requirement is for us to believe in God's Son, Jesus Christ, and accept Him as our Lord and Savior. The Bible tells us that "God so loved the world, that he gave His only begotten Son, that whosoever believeth in him should not perish, but have everlasting life" (John 3:16). Romans 10:9 tells us that "if thou shalt confess with thy mouth the Lord Jesus, and shalt believe in thine heart that God hath raised him from the dead, thou shalt be saved." In the Holy Bible, Jesus Christ said that "I am the way, the truth, and the life; no man cometh unto the Father, but by me" (John 14:6). When we hear and believe the gospel and accept Jesus Christ as our Lord and Savior, we are born again, and after salvation, we are now expected to grow in Christ and develop a closer personal relationship with God by (1) spending time with God, (2) studying God's Word, and (3) communication with God through prayer.

Spending Time with God

When we hear the gospel, believe and accept Jesus Christ as our Lord and Savior, we are born again. Now we can grow in Christ and develop a personal relationship with God by (1) spending time with God, (2) studying God's Word, and (3) communicating with God through prayer.

Spending quiet time alone with God is an important and necessary step to take in order to gain a better understanding of God. Spending quality time with God enables us to grow and mature as saints. In our efforts to get to know God better, it is imperative that we spend time with Him and develop a closer personal relationship with Him. In the natural, if we want to get to know someone better or have a closer relationship, then it is essential for us to spend quality time with that individual. Likewise, spiritually, we should spend quality time with God if we want to draw closer to Him.

There are many ways that we can draw closer to God, such as obeying God, being led by the Holy Spirit, reading God's Word, praying, seeking God early, and attending church.

When we are born again, the Holy Spirit lives within us. In getting to know God better, it is vital for us to be obedient to the leading of the Holy Spirit. The Bible tells us, that as Christians, we should know the voice of the Lord and should not follow any other (John 10:4-5). As we spend time with God and grow closer to Him we will learn to listen attentively for God, know His voice, and follow his lead. God still speaks to us today, and when He does speak, we should listen to Him. God speaks to us in so many different ways. He speaks to us through His Word, by His servants, by His Spirit, His angels, dreams, and in many other situations and circumstances (Hebrews 1:1-2; Exodus 9:1; Jonah 1:1; Matthew 1:20-21, 2:22; Acts 10:10-28; Luke 1:11-12, 26-27, 2:8-10).

We learn more of God when we spend time in His Word. Reading God's Word is an excellent way to draw closer to God because we become more familiar with Him and His ways. In the Word, we can see the love God has toward us. The Word show how God's grace and mercy are every present for us. The Word of God is true and will last forever (1 Peter 1:25).

We can spend time with God in prayer. Jesus Christ frequently sought God early in prayer. The Bible tells us that Jesus rose early to pray, He fasted and prayed, and He frequently went off alone to pray (Mark 1:35; Matthew 4:14, 14:23). We too should seek God early, fast and pray. God is a jealous God, and He wants to be first in all things (Exodus 34:14). God wants to be first in our lives, and by beginning our day with God, is just one way we can try to meet this expectation that God has for us. When we start our day seeking God, we are putting Him first, and we are doing things God's way. Starting our day with God sets the tone for the rest of the day, because when we start our day with God, it will help us to have a good day. When we start anything with God, it will always make it better and more successful. God is awesome and He will help us in all our endeavors if we ask Him. Praising and worshiping God, giving thanks unto Him, and morning devotion are other important activities we can do to draw closer to God and get to know Him. It pleases God when we start our day by acknowledging Him and thanking Him for all the many wonderful blessings He has given us.

Spending time with God, prepares us to face the world and meet our daily challenges. We can get up early in the morning and pray, read the Word, and stay in an attitude of prayer all day; doing this will help us to have an enjoyable day. When we regularly spend time with God, we will develop a closer walk with the Lord. When setting aside time and place to be with God, we should select a specific place and time to meet with Him. We should select an area where we won't be distracted by outside noise or people. The Bible tells us in Matthew 6:33 to "seek ye first the kingdom of God, and his righteousness; and all these things shall be added unto you." God owns everything and He will give us all the things that we may need in life, but we are to seek Him and not the things. When we seek God, we will find Him because Jesus Christ is available to all mankind. Developing a closer walk with God is a personal decision that we make.

The lives we are living today are the product of our own previous behavior and decisions. Our present and past actions help determine the rate of our spiritual growth and the state of our current spiritual condition. So, if you are feeling alone, weak, or powerless, my question is: "What have you been doing, saying or thinking?" If we remain faithful in our walk with God, we will continue to grow and developed a closer relationship with Him. When we are faithful and committed to God and are consistent in prayer and studying His Word, our faith will increase because faith comes by hearing the Word of God (Romans 10:17). God's Word tells us that God will never leave us nor forsake us and that He will always be with us even to the end of the world (Hebrews 13:5; Matthew 28:20). The Word tells us that God loves those who love Him and those that seek Him early will find Him (Proverbs 8:17).

We can learn more about God when we attend a Bible-believing, and Bible-teaching church that is led by a true man of God. Proverbs 8:34-36 tell us that "blessed is the man that heareth me, watching daily at my gates, waiting at the post of my doors. For whoso findeth me findeth life, and shall obtain favor of the Lord. But he that sinneth against me wrongeth his own soul: all they that hate me love death." There is no place I would rather be than in the presence of the Lord.

B. B. Hicks

Studying God's Word

When we hear the gospel, believe, and accept Jesus Christ as our Lord and Savior we are born again. Now we can grow in Christ and develop a personal relationship with God by (1) spending time with God, (2) studying God's Word, and (3) communicating with God through prayer.

The Bible tells us to "Study to shew thyself approved unto God, a workman that needeth not to be ashamed, rightly dividing the word of truth" (2 Timothy 2:15). In our efforts to gain a better understanding of God, we should not only spend quiet time with God but also spend time studying and reading God's Word. When we read the Bible, we can increase our knowledge about God. "For the Lord giveth wisdom: out of His mouth cometh knowledge and understanding" (Proverbs 2:6). The Bible is true and is a compilation of the inspired Word of God. The Bible tells us that "all Scripture is given by inspiration of God, and is profitable for doctrine, for reproof, for correction, for instruction in righteousness: that the man of God may be perfect, thoroughly furnished unto all good works" (2 Timothy 3: 16-17). The Word of God is forever "settled in heaven and the entrance of God's Word giveth light; it giveth understanding to the simple" (Psalm 119:89, 130). In reading the Bible, we can learn about God the Father, Jesus Christ, His Son; and the Holy Ghost and how the three operate as one. The Bible tells us that it was God who created the heaven and the earth and that He created everything that was created (John 1:3). Reading the Bible is necessary in getting to know God. In John

1:1 we find written that in the beginning was the Word and the Word was with God and the Word was God. So, when you are spending time in the Word, you are actually spending time with God.

Many people are led astray when the Word of God is distorted or altered by people who profess to be men and women of God, but who may be more concerned with pleasing people than with telling the whole truth of the gospel. Hosea 4:6 tells us how God's people are destroyed for lack of knowledge. But when we study the Word and get to know the Word for ourselves, we should not be deceived by these individuals because we will be able to distinguish the truth from lies. When we study the Word, we will be able to identify these individuals and move on because the Bible tells us to "mark and avoid those who cause divisions and offenses that are contrary to the doctrine that was learned" (Romans 16:17).

The Bible says that, "as for God, His way is perfect: the Word of the Lord is tried: he is a buckler to all those that trust in Him" (Psalm 18:30). Everything we read in the Bible is true, and if God said it, then it will surely come to pass. God's Word will not return to Him void – it will accomplish what God meant for it to do (Isaiah 55:11). God's Word provides direction, guidance, and it gives life, insight, and wisdom. "For the word of God is quick, and powerful, and sharper than any twoedged sword, piercing even to the dividing asunder of soul and spirit, and of the joints and morrow, and is a discerner of the thoughts and intents of the heart" (Hebrews 4:12). The Bible tells us that the Word of God is a lamp unto our feet and a light unto our path (Psalm 119:105).

The Word of God is our road map to help us navigate righteously through life.

King David said, "Thy word have I hid in mine heart, that I might not sin against thee" (Psalm 119:11). Whatever we need can be found in the Word of God because there is nothing new under the sun (Ecclesiastes 1:9). In the Bible, we can find love stories, stories of failures, successes, war, murder, death, suicide, friendship, deceit, betrayal, prophets, false prophets, Satan, angels, hell, heaven, laws, commandment, miracles, grace, God's plan for salvation, love, hatred, and stories of the willing sacrifice Jesus Christ made for us on the cross. This list is not all-inclusive for there are so many more subjects that can be found in the Word of God. In the Word we learn of creation, the flood, and of the children of Israel who were God's chosen people. We can also read how the Gentiles, who was once on the outside, became engrafted into the promises of God (Ephesians 2:11-22, 3:6). We can read about the many different people who were used by God to accomplish His purpose, plans, and desires for their lives. We can get a better understanding of God through His Word. In studying God's Word, we will also learn about the nature and characteristic of God. The Word shows us how God loves, forgives, has compassion, and provides grace and mercy. The Word reveals who God is and how He operates. God is "the Almighty God" (Genesis 17:1). God is the "Alpha and Omega, the beginning and the ending" (Revelation 1:8). He is the great "I AM," "the King eternal, immortal, invisible, the only wise God" (Exodus 3:14; 1 Timothy 1:17). God is love (1 John 4:8). It is shown in the Holy Scriptures how God manifested Himself to many different individuals and how His character was made known to them. These individuals left their encounter with God able to see God in a brand new and totally different way than they did before their interaction with God. When we read the Bible, we will find the story of the fall of mankind and his subsequent separation from God. Because of this fall/separation, God sent His only begotten Son into this world to save us from our sins. Jesus Christ, because of His great love for us and out of obedience to His Father, freely gave His life and died on the cross for us. Jesus could have so easily come down from the cross, for He had a legion of angels ready to act on His command. But because of His great love for us, He kept Himself bound to the cross. Jesus gave His life so that we might live. Jesus said that "no man taketh it from me, but I lay it down of myself. I have power to lay it down and I have power to take it again" (John 10:18). Jesus Christ freely died for us, so we ought to freely live for Him. In the Word, we find it written that Jesus said that "the thief cometh not, but for to steal, and to kill and to destroy: I am come that they might have life, and that they might have it more abundantly" (John 10:10).

It is a good thing when we come into the full knowledge of Jesus Christ, when we get to know Him as our Lord and Savior. When we get to know God through His Word, it will help us to make sense of this world and provide meaning and purpose for our lives. Without Jesus Christ in our lives, we are condemned to live a meaningless, hopeless life in this world where the final outcome is death and destruction. But with God, we have a brighter future in store for us. Heaven is available to all those who believe on God's Son and His Word. When we choose to believe and accept Jesus Christ, we now have a purpose, a promise of eternal life after death, and a better place to live than on earth – that place is heaven. The knowledge of God gives us hope for a better tomorrow because the Word shows us that the troubles of this world are not forever. The Bible tells us everything we need to know about how to live a victorious life in Christ.

God's plan of salvation is made known to us as we read the Word of God. By reading the Word, we learn about being born again. The gospel is the good news of Jesus Christ, who is our Lord and Savior. Salvation is being born again or being saved from our sins. Believing and accepting Jesus as our Lord and Savior; becoming part of the body of Christ, saves us from the second death, hell and destruction, and it gives us the ability to live eternally with God in heaven. This salvation is free and available to all men.

When we are exposed to the gospel or the good news of Jesus Christ, it enables us to recognize or realize the sinful condition that we are in without Jesus Christ in our lives.

When we read or hear the gospel or the truth of God and of His Son, Jesus Christ, we can either believe or disbelieve this information. We can repent, turn away from our sins and turn to Christ, asking Him to come into our hearts and be our Lord and Savior. When we do this, we then become a part of the body of Christ. That is when we believe in our hearts and confess with our mouths that Jesus is our Lord and Savior. When we believe and accept the gospel as the truth, we believe that Jesus is the Son of God, who died on the cross for our sins but rose again on the third day. Jesus Christ is now sitting on the right hand of the Father in heaven making intercession for us. The Holy Scriptures tell us that when we are born again, we are new creatures in Christ and become a part of a new family in the body of Christ (2 Corinthians 5:17).

The Bible tells us that the end will not come until everyone has had an opportunity to hear the gospel (Matthew 24:14). As new converts, we are babies in Christ, and we must continue to grow and develop a personal relationship with God.

We can get to know God better when we spend time in the Word and pray, which is communicating with God. The Word of God let us know that we are to commune with God on a regular basis and be obedient to His voice (Luke 18:1; Romans 8:14). When we get to know God, we will have confidence (trust) that God will do just what His Word says He will do. When we trust God, believe in Him and take Him at His Word, we will be able to stand on His promises no matter what the circumstance. Even in the face of adversity, when there is no way out, we will be able to say; "I know my God is able to help me." It is the knowing, the trusting in God that saves us every time. When we draw closer to God, we will develop a closer personal relationship with Him. When we read the Bible, communicate to Him in prayer, and follow the leading of the Holy Spirit, we will also grow closer to God. When we read the Word of God, we must believe God's Word. Faith comes by hearing the Word of God. We can also get to know God better by observing how He works things out on our behalf. Our answered prayers help increase our faith because if He did it once, He'll do it again.

A wonderful way to see or experience God is through His creation in nature. The Word tells us that it was God who made the trees, wind, sun, moon, stars, day, and night. There is a greater power, something greater than man, which is God, the Almighty. In studying God's Word, we can see the manifestation of God in many different ways. The Word lets us know that God is the true and living and only wise God.

When we study the Word, it will be beneficial for us if we ask God to help us understand what we are reading. We can also ask Him to help us apply His Word, to our lives. What I frequently hear stated in my church is "the Bible is God's Word speaking to us." By studying God's Word, we can learn about the many men and women of God, who God used for His glory and purpose. We can gain a better understanding of God when we attend a Bible-believing, Bible-teaching church. Attending Bible study on a regular basis will also help us to increase our knowledge of God. In Bible study we have opportunities to ask all those unanswered questions that we can't ask during Sunday morning services. Bible study is a wonderful place to get clarification and insight on various biblical subjects. It is excellent for us to study God's Word, but it is more excellent to be doers of the Word because God wants us to be not only a hearer of the Word but a doer of the Word (James 1:22-25).

Reading the Bible can teach us more about:
1. The fall of mankind
2. Why we needed a Savior

3. Jesus' descension to earth
4. Jesus' ascension to heaven
5. Judgment, great white throne
6. Hell, lake of fire
7. Jesus's return, the day of wrath, heaven, (rapture; meeting Jesus in the air)
8. Satan, the author of lies

Communicating with God through Prayer

When we hear the gospel, believe, and accept Jesus Christ as our Lord and Savior we are born again. Now we can grow in Christ and develop a personal relationship with God by (1) spending time with God, (2) studying God's Word, and (3) communicating with God through prayer.

Prayer is communicating with God. Prayer is a person talking to God. Communicating with God through prayer is one way to build a closer relationship with Him. If we want to get to know God better, then we should spend time with Him in prayer. The Bible tells us to "Be careful for nothing; but in everything by prayer and supplication with thanksgiving let your requests be made known unto God" (Philippians 4:6). We can make requests, petitions, ask for God's help, offer Him praise, thanksgiving, or just inform Him of our needs and problems. We are to pray for the lost, sick, pastors, saints, children, poor, motherless, fatherless, government, our nation, family, friends, and even for our enemies. We can pray about anything and everything. We can pray about our every concern. God hears us when we pray (1 John 5:14). The Bible tells us that we have not because we ask not (James 4:2). Our prayers can be long or short, done privately or publicly, but all are our effort to communicate with our God. In order for us to have effective communication with God, we must listen for Him during our time in prayer. We are to pray to God the Father in the name of His Son, Jesus Christ (John 16:22-24, 14:13-14). When we pray we are communicating with a God who is all powerful, all knowing and is everywhere. God already knows what we need before we ask Him, but He wants us to ask (Matthew 6:8).

In Matthew 6:5-8, Jesus Christ teaches His disciples how to pray and gives us specific instructions on prayer. We get results and answered prayers from God when we pray in faith and according to the will of God because He hears us when we pray and answers our prayers (James 1:6-7; 1 John 5:14-15). We should pray with the right motive (James 4:2-3; Matthew 6:5-7). We should not be prideful or boastful when we pray (Luke 18:9-14). We must pray in faith and not waver or doubt if we want to receive anything from God (James 5:13-15; James 1: 6-7). We must forgive in order to be forgiven of God (Matthew 6:14-15). We are to pray regularly and sincerely (Psalm 55:17; Daniel 6:10, 9:20; Job 1:1-5; Luke 2:36-37; Acts 10:1-2; James 5:16). We are to pray about everything and worry about nothing (Philippians 4:6-5). We are to pray without ceasing, to continue in prayer, and we are to pray for authority, because this is God's will for us and prayerlessness is sin (1 Thessalonians 5:17; Ephesians 5:18; 1 Timothy 2; Matthew 6:5-13;1 Samuel 12:23). We are to pray for the peace of Jerusalem (Psalm 122:6). "The prayer of faith shall save the sick" (James 5:15-16). Jesus said my house shall be called the house of prayer (Matthew 21:13). The Bible tells us to "Confess your faults one to another, and pray one for another that ye may be healed. The effectual fervent prayer of a righteous man availeth much" (James 5:16). Jesus Christ instructs His disciples on prayer and gave them specific instructions on how to pray and on how not to pray. Jesus gives us an example on how to pray in Matthew 6:5-13. In these Holy Scriptures Jesus Christ let us know that our motive must be pure in prayer and we should not behave like the hypocrites. We are not to pray to be seen or for show. Jesus tells us that when we pray in private, we should go into our closet and shut the door. He also tells us when we pray in private, God will openly reward us. Jesus further let us know that when we pray, we are not to keep repeating or saying the same thing over and over. Jesus doesn't want us to pray as the unlearned or ungodly, using vain repetitions, because He tells us that God already knows what we have need of before we ask Him. After Jesus instructs His disciples on what not to do when praying, He then tells them how to pray:

We are to start our prayer by acknowledging God for who He is:

> *Our Father which art in heaven, Hallowed be thy name (Matthew 6:9)*

Next, we are to come into agreement with God's will:

> *Thy kingdom come. Thy will be done in earth, as it is in heaven (Matthew 6:10)*

We then make a request for our physical needs of the Father:

> *Give us this day our daily bread (Matthew 6:11)*

We then make a request for our spiritual needs:

> *And forgive us our debts, as we forgive our debtors (Matthew 6:12).*

Finally, we are to make a request for God to keep and deliver us and we are to acknowledge God's perpetual ownership of the kingdom, the power and the glory:

> *And lead us not into temptation, but deliver us from evil: For thine is the Kingdom, and the power, and the glory, for ever. Amen. (Matthew 6:13).*

Selected Prayers Found in the Holy Bible
(this list is not all-inclusive)

The Prayer of Abraham's Servant (Genesis 24:12-15): Abraham's eldest servant was sent to find a wife for his son Issac: Rebekah.

Hannah's Prayer (1 Samuel 1:1-17): Wife of Elkanah was barren. While she prayed to God, Eli thought she was drunk. Eli later told her that God would grant her petition.

Hezekiah's Prayer (2 Kings 20:1-6): Hezekiah was sick unto death. The prophet Isaiah told Hezekiah that the Lord said for him to set his house in order because he would surely die. Hezekiah turned his face to the wall and prayed and was healed and God granted him another fifteen years.

King Jehoshaphat (2 Chronicles 20:1-18): A great multitude came upon Judah to battle. The king prayed, and God answered his prayer. King Jehoshaphat was told not to be afraid or dismayed of the great multitude, because the battle is not His but was God's.

Jesus Christ (John 17): Jesus Christ prayed for His disciples, and for us who will believe in Jesus through their words.

God wants to hear from us in prayer. Just like an earthly father wants to hear from his children; God our heavenly father wants to hear from us, His children, in prayer.

The Lord is always available for us to call on, and He hears us when we pray (Matthew 28:20; Isaiah 65:24; Psalm 145:18). God is never too busy for us (Hebrews 13:5**).** First John 5:14 says, "And this in the confidence that we have in him, that, if we ask any thing according to his will, he heareth us: And if we know that he hears us, whatsoever we ask, we know that we have the petitions that we desired of him." When we draw near unto God, He in turn will draw near unto us (James 4:8). Matthew 7:7 tells us to "ask and it shall be given unto you; seek and ye shall find; knock, and it shall be opened unto you." Jesus Christ is our perfect role model for all things and one of the many examples He provides is how He spent time alone with God in prayer (Matthew14:23, 26:36; Mark 6:46, 1:35; Luke 5:16, 9:18). Jesus Christ came to earth with a God given purpose and a plan for His life, and although He was on a mission from God, He still took the time to communicate with His Father in prayer. The Word tells us that those who seek Him early shall find Him and that we should seek the Lord while He may be found and to call on Him while He is near (Proverbs 8:17; Isaiah 55:6).

The Bible shows how Jesus rose early to pray, how He fasted and prayed, and how He frequently went off alone to pray (Mark 1:35; Matthew 4:14, 14:23). As believers, we too must spend time communicating with God in prayer. There are many times when we pray that we do all the talking and don't take time to listen to what God has to say. Effective communication takes place when one person speaks and the other person listens and vice versa. If we want a closer relationship with God, then we should take time to listen to Him.

God is able to "do exceeding abundantly above all that we ask or think, according to the power that worketh in us," (Ephesians 3:20). We are to come to God in prayer and we are to continue to pray without ceasing because the Bible tells us that men ought to always pray (1 Thessalonians 5:17; Luke 18:1). Jesus said, "Whatsoever ye shall ask the Father in my name, he will give it you. Hitherto have ye asked nothing in my name; ask, and ye shall receive, that your joy may be full" (John 16:23-24). We are to pray to God in faith, expecting results and expecting answers to our prayers, because Hebrews 11:6 tells us that without faith it is impossible to please God, and those who come to Him must believe that He is and that He is a rewarder of those who diligently seek Him. "Let us therefore come boldly to the throne room of grace, that we may obtain mercy, and find grace to help in the time of need" (Hebrews 4:16). Spending time communicating with God in prayer is pivotal in getting to know God.

Getting to Know God through Scripture

The earth is the Lord's, and the fullness thereof; the world, and they that dwell therein. For he hath founded it upon the seas, and established it upon the floods. Who shall ascend into the hill of the Lord? or who shall stand in his holy place? He that hath clean hands, and a pure heart; who hath not lifted up his soul unto vanity, nor sworn deceitfully. He shall receive the blessing of the Lord, and righteousness from the God of his salvation. This is the generation of them that seek him, that seek thy face, O Jacob. Selah. Lift up your heads, O ye gates;

and be ye lift up, ye everlasting doors; and the King of glory shall come in. Who is this King of glory? The Lord strong and mighty, the Lord mighty in battle. Lift up your heads, O ye gates; even lift them up, ye everlasting doors; and the King of glory shall come in. Who is this King of glory? The Lord of host, he is the King of glory. Selah. (Psalm 24)

Chapter 2

Trusting God

What does it mean to trust God? We are trusting God when we believe God and have confidence in Him and His Word. Trusting means that we have faith in God, knowing that we can depend on Him. It means that we believe God can do whatever His Word says He will do.

The Bible tell us in Hebrews 11:1 that 'now faith is the substance of things hoped for, the evidence of things not seen." We are to walk by faith and not by sight (2 Corinthians 5:11). The Holy Scriptures also let us know that "without faith it is impossible to please him: for he that cometh to God must believe that he is, and that he is a rewarder of them that diligently seek him" (Hebrews 11:6-7). We should be able to see that trusting God means that we are to rely on Him, believe Him or have confidence in Him. It means that we have the belief that God will do whatever His Word says He will do. Trust is to believe God. Those who believe and have accepted Jesus Christ as their Lord and Savior are expected to have faith, trust in the Lord, and to believe in His Word. We are to have faith in our God. He will do just what His Word says He will do. God is who His Word says He is. "God is not like man that he would lie" (Numbers 23:19). If God said it, He will bring it to pass. God's Word will not return unto Him void (Isaiah 55:11). God thoughts and ways are much higher than our thoughts and ways, as high as the heaven is to the earth (Isaiah 55:8-9). We have to get the doubt and wavering out of our hearts and minds and just believe God and His Word (James 1:6-8).

The Bible tells us that "faith cometh by hearing and hearing by the Word of God" (Romans 10:17). When we have faith, we believe God and His Word. "Every word of God is pure: he is a shield unto them that put their trust in him" (Proverbs 30:5). Scripture tells us that we are to ask God for what we need, but we are to ask in faith and not doubt or waver, because if we doubt, we will not receive anything from God (James 1:6-7). The Word says that "Blessed is the man who maketh the Lord his trust" (Psalm 40: 4). We can trust God to take care of us and all our needs. When we are born again, Jesus Christ becomes our safe harbor from the storms of life. Jesus Christ has redeemed us from the curse of the law, and we are to put our trust in Him. Developing a closer relationship with God helps us to trust Him more. We become closer to God as we commune with Him on a regular basis, are obedient to His Word, listen, and obey the voice of God. Once we get a better understanding of God, we will have confidence that God will do just what His Word said He will do. When this happens, we are trusting and believing God. "It is better to trust in the Lord than to put confidence in man" (Psalms 118:8). People can and will let you down or lie to you, but God will never let us down. It is impossible for God to lie because whatever God says, whether good or bad, will come to past. God is good, just and righteous (Psalm 143:10-11). The Bible tells us to "trust in the Lord with all thine heart; and lean not unto thine own understanding. In all thy ways acknowledge him, and he will direct our paths" (Proverbs 3:5-6). We are to continue with God and trust Him for all things. Matthew 6:33 tells us to seek God first and He will add all the things we may need in life. God is concerned about what we are concerned about. There is nothing too hard for God. What is impossible with man is always possible with God. God is a miracle worker, a problem solver, a way maker. God is all we need; He is the great I AM. In Him we can find the answer to every problem in life that may come our way. If you need good health, wealth, peace, or joy, God's got it. The Bible tells us we have not because we ask not (James 4:2). Trusting in God should be easy because His record or reputation speaks for itself. He has never failed, never lost a case, never left us nor forsaken us (Isaiah 41:10-13; Hebrews 13:5). He is with us always even to the end of the world (Matthew 28:20). We are to have faith in God. The Bible tells us that our faith can move mountains if we don't doubt in our hearts but believe (Mark 11:22-24). As believers in Christ, we are to believe God and take Him at His Word. We must not doubt, but we are to trust in God, and we are to believe and depend on Him.

As saints, we are to believe God and take Him at His Word. We must not doubt or waver in our faith, our minds or our hearts. We are to just believe God and His Word, because God's Word tells us that without faith, it is impossible to please God. Those who come to Him must believe that He is and that He is a rewarder of those who diligently seek Him (Hebrews 11:6). We must have faith in God to receive anything from God. In the natural economic system, we need money to obtain desired items or services. In the spiritual realm, all we need to use is our faith to receive our desires and/ or request from God. It is for this reason, that you will find it written in the Holy Bible the Scripture verses that state, "According to your faith be it unto you" or the verse that says that "thy faith hath made thee whole" (Matthew 9:29; Mark 5:34, 10:52; Luke 17:19). The Holy Scriptures let us know that faith the size of a mustard seed can move a tree (Luke 17:6). The Bible teaches us that God is truth, reliable, and dependable (Numbers 23:19). We have faith in God when we believe in God and His Word. We have faith in God when we trust God and take Him at His Word. We have confidence in God and His abilities to do whatever He promised to do. Therefore, "Let us hold fast the profession of our faith without wavering (for he is faithful that promised)" (Hebrews 10:23).

Abel: by faith offered God a more excellent sacrifice than Cain

Enoch: by faith was translated that he should not see death

Noah: by faith being warned of God of things not seen as yet, moved with fear, prepared an ark

Abraham: by faith when he was called to go out into a place which he should after receive for an inheritance, obeyed

Sara: by faith received strength to conceive seed, because she judged him faithful who promised

Abraham: by faith, when he was tried, offered up Isaac' and he that had received the promises offered up his only begotten son

Isaac: by faith blessed Jacob and Esau concerning things to come

Jacob: by faith when he was dying, blessed both sons of Joseph; worshipped, leaning upon the top of his staff

Joseph: by faith, when he died, made mention of the departing of the children of Israel; and gave commandment concerning his bones

Moses: by faith, when he was come to years, refused to be called the son of Pharaoh's daughter;

Children of Israel: by faith they passed through the Red Sea as by dry land

Wall of Jericho: by faith the wall of Jericho fell down

Rahab: by faith the harlot Rahab perished not with them that believed not, when she had received the spies with peace. - Hebrews 11: 4-31

In Mark 11:22-23, Jesus says to "Have faith in God. For verily I say unto you, That whosoever shall say unto this mountain, Be thou removed, and be thou cast into the sea; and shall not doubt in his heart, but shall believe that those things which he saith shall come to pass; he shall have whatsoever he saith." It is our faith that causes us to receive from God and this includes salvation, and all the other promises of God. The Holy Scripture Romans 5:1-2 states: "Therefore being justified by faith, we have peace with God through our Lord Jesus Christ: By whom we have access by faith into this grace wherein we stand, and rejoice in hope of the glory of God." We must have faith in God. We must believe God and believe His Word.

We must have confidence in God and in His abilities to do whatever He promised to do.

> "For whatsoever is born of God overcometh the world: and this is the victory that overcometh the world, even our faith. Who is he that overcometh the world, but he that believeth that Jesus is the Son of God?" (1 John 5:4).

We are victorious in Christ when we believe God and His written Word. On this Christian journey we are to "walk by faith and not by sight" because faith is the substance of things hoped for, the evidence of things not seen" (2 Corinthians 5:7; Hebrews 11:1).

Trusting God through Scripture

He that dwelleth in the secret place of the most High shall abide under the shadow of the Almighty. I will say of the Lord, He is my refuge and my fortress: my God; in him will I trust. Surely he shall deliver thee from the snare of the fowler, and from the noisome pestilence. He shall cover thee with his feathers, and under his wings shalt thou trust: his truth shall be thy shield and buckler. Thou shalt not be afraid for the terror by night; nor for the arrow that flieth by day; Nor for the pestilence that walketh in darkness; nor for the destruction that wasteth at noonday. A thousand shall fall at thy side, and ten thousand at thy right hand; but is shall not come nigh thee. Only with thine eyes shalt thou behold and see the reward of the wicked. Because thou hast made the Lord, which is my refuge, even the most High, thy habitation; There shall no evil befall thee, neither shall any plague come nigh thy dwelling. For he shall give his angels charge over thee, to keep thee in all thy ways. They shall bear thee up in their hands, lest thou dash thy foot against a stone. Thou shalt tread upon the lion and adder: the young lion and the dragon shalt thou trample under feet. Because he hath set his love upon me, therefore will I deliver him: I will set him on high, because he hath known my name. He shall call upon me, and I will answer him; I will be with him in trouble; I will deliver him, and honour him. With long life will I satisfy him, and shew him my salvation. (Psalm 91)

Psalm 4:5: Offer the sacrifices of righteousness, and put your trust in the Lord,

Isaiah 26:4: Trust ye in the Lord for ever: for in the Lord JEHOVAH is everlasting strength:

Psalm 18:2: The Lord is my rock, and my fortress, and my deliverer; my God, my strength, in whom I will trust; my buckler, and the horn of my salvation, and my high tower.

Psalm 18:30: As for God, his way is perfect: the word of the Lord is tried: he is a buckler to all those that trust in him.

Nahum 1:7: The Lord is good, a strong hold in the day of trouble; and he knoweth them that trust in him.

Jeremiah 17:7: Blessed in the man that trusteth in the Lord, and whose hope is the Lord is.

Psalm 5:11-12: But let all those that put their trust in thee rejoice: let them ever shout for joy, because thou defendest them: let them also that love thy name be joyful in thee.

Psalm 32:10: Many sorrows shall be to the wicked: but he that trusteth in the Lord, mercy shall compass him about,

Psalm 7:1: O Lord my God, in thee do I put my trust: save me from all them that persecute me, and deliver me:

Psalm 16:1: Preserve me, O God; for in thee do I put my trust.

Psalm 9:10: And they that know thy name will put their trust in thee: for thou, Lord, hast not forsaken them that seek thee.

Hebrews 11:1: Now faith is the substance of things hoped for, the evidence of thing not seen.

Hebrews 11:6: But without faith it is impossible to please him: for he that cometh to God must believe that he is, and that he is a rewarder of them that diligently seek him.

Hebrews 11:32-34: And what shall I more say? For the time would fail me to tell of Gedeon, and of Barak, and of Samson, and of Jephthae, of David also, and Samuel, and of the prophets who through faith subdued kingdoms, wrought righteousness, obtained promises, stopped the mouth of lions, quenched the violence of fire, escaped the edge of the sword, out of weakness were made strong, waxed valiant in fight, turned to flight the armies of the aliens.

Chapter 3

Turning Back to God

When looking at America's history, you will find that God was the solid rock of this nation's foundation. But some have left their first love and are living and falling for anything. We are now living in a time when people are calling what is right wrong and what is wrong right. A time when what is good and moral is now unacceptable and is being called wrong, unkind, or not politically correct. Our land needs healing! We are living in a time where anything goes, a time when people are willing to compromise on their moral or religious belief in exchange for a promising career or fitting in with the "in" crowd. We are living in a time when our children are no longer safe in their schools, on the bus, or walking home from school. Our children are sometimes not even safe in their own homes, because they have at their finger-tips access to malicious, or inappropriate information and people on social media. We are living during a time when there is an increase of confusion and strife. A time when lies are running rampant in our society and are tolerated and accepted as normal. We are living during a time when hatred is openly expressed and is prevalent in our community. Our land needs healing!

According to God's Word, He is ready, willing, and able to heal our land, but it is up to us. There are conditions that must be met. There is something that we need to do in order to obtain this healing. The Word of God says that "if my people, which are called by my name, shall humble themselves, and pray, and seek my face, and turn from their wicked ways; then will I hear from heaven, and will forgive their sin and will heal their land." (2 Chronicles 7:14).

I'm calling for all saints, as well as our nation, to turn back to God. I am calling for all people to turn to God. Our land needs healing. If you don't believe me, then watch the six o'clock news. You will hear of the killing, stealing, drugs, abuse, crime, lies, white-collar crimes, and child abductions where the child is later found raped and murdered. Our land needs healing! It is well past time to take a stand, and if you be for God, then say so. It is time to say, "As for me and my house we will serve the Lord!" (Joshua 24:15). Additionally, in the book of Joshua, the people were told that "if it seems evil unto you to serve the Lord, choose you this day whom ye will serve; whether the gods which your fathers served that were on the other side of the flood, or the gods of the Amorites, in whose land ye dwell:" (Joshua 24:15). We all have to choose who we are going to serve. Indecision is a decision in and of itself. We must purposely choose to believe the gospel and ask Jesus Christ to be our Lord and Savior.

This is also a call for those who are lost and don't know Jesus as their Lord and Savior.

It is a call for the lost to turn to the only true and living God. The only way to God is through His Son, Jesus Christ. Jesus said in the Holy Bible, "I am the way, the truth and the life: no man cometh unto the Father but by me" (John 14:6). Therefore, based on these facts, if you don't know Jesus and want to get to know Him, you can because salvation is free and available to all who will believe in Jesus Christ, the Son of God. Scripture tells us, "The fool hath said in his heart, There is no God" (Psalm 14:1; 53:1).

Some of you may already be saved, you may know God and trust Him, but for whatever reason you have found yourself in a backslidden condition. You can turn back or come back to God. The Bible tells us that if we do sin, we have an advocate with the Father, Christ Jesus, who makes intercession for us to the Father (1 John 2:1). The Holy Scriptures lets us know that God doesn't want us to sin, but it tells us that if we do He will forgive and cleanse us. "If we confess our sins, he is faithful and just to forgive us our sins and to cleanse us of all unrighteousness" (1 John 1:9). God loves all His people and wants all men to be saved, and to come into the knowledge of truth (1 Timothy 2:3-4). The Word also says that "the Lord is not slack concerning his promise, as some men count slackness; but is longsuffering to us-ward, not willing that any should perish, but that all should come to repentance" (2 Peter 3:9). God forgives our sin and remembers them no more and He will cast our sins as far as the east is from the west (Isaiah 43:25; Hebrews 8:12; Psalm 103:12). Therefore, if you are out of fellowship with God, you can always come back to God. Once we repent or turn away from our sins and ask God to forgive us of our sins, we are back in right standing with God. We can return home to God just as the prodigal son did when he came to himself and realized his awful condition. He admitted what he had done, he returned to his father, and likewise, we too can repent of our sins and return to our Father. He will welcome us with open arms (Luke 15:11-24). King David also repented of his sins after he was shown the error of his ways by the prophet Nathan. King David confessed his sins to God and repented of his sins (2 Samuel 12; Psalm 51). The Bible tells us, "there is joy in the presence of the angels of God over one sinner that repenteth" (Luke15:10). We all have been afforded the same option to repent of our sins and return or come to God, because of what Jesus Christ did for us. By reason of Christ, salvation is free and available to all who will believe on Him.

"As ye have therefore received Christ Jesus the Lord, so walk ye in him (Colossians 2:6).

We should not turn back, quit, or give up but we are to stay connected with God.

Turning Back to God through Scripture

Have mercy upon me, O God, according to thy lovingkindness; according unto the multitude of thy tender mercies blot out my transgressions. Wash me thoroughly from mine iniquity, and cleanse me from my sin. For I acknowledge my transgressions: and my sin is ever before me. Against thee, thee only, have I sinned, and done evil in thy sight: that thou mightiest be justified when thou speakest, and be clear when thou judgest. Behold, I was shapen in iniquity; and in sin did my mother conceive me. Behold, thou desirest truth in the inward parts: and in the hidden part thou shalt make me to know wisdom. Purge me with hyssop, and I shall be clean: wash me, and I shall be whiter than snow. Make me to hear joy and gladness; that the bones which thou hath broken may rejoice. Hide thy face from my sins, and blot out all mine iniquities. Create in me a clean heart, O God; and renew a right spirit within me. Cast me not away from thy presence; and take not thy holy spirit from me. Restore unto me the joy of thy salvation; and uphold me with thy free spirit. Then will I teach transgressors thy ways; and sinners shall be converted unto thee. Deliver me from bloodguiltiness, O God, thou God of my salvation: and my tongue shall sing aloud of thy righteousness. O Lord, open thou my lips; and my mouth shall shew forth thy praise. For thou desirest not sacrifice; else would I give it: thou delightest not in burnt offering. The sacrifices of God are a broken spirit: a broken and a contrite heart, O God thou wilt not despise. Do good in thy good pleasure unto Zion: build thou the wall of Jerusalem. Then shalt thou be pleased with the sacrifices of righteousness, with burnt offering and whole burnt offering: then shall they offer bullocks upon thine altar. (Psalm 51)

***

That which was from the beginning, which we have heard, which we have seen with our eyes, which we have looked upon, and our hands have handled, of the Word of life; (For the life was manifested, and we have seen it, and bear witness, and shew unto you that eternal life, which was with the Father, and was manifested unto us;). That which we have seen and heard declare we unto you, that ye also may have fellowship with us; and truly our fellowship is with the Father, and with his Son Jesus Christ. And these things write we unto you, that your joy may be full. This then is the message which we have heard of him, and declare unto you, that God is light, and in him is no darkness at all. If we say that we have fellowship with him, and walk in darkness, we lie, and do not the truth: But if we walk in the light, as he is in the light, we have fellowship one with another, and the blood of Jesus Christ his Son cleanseth us from all sin. If we say we have no sin, we deceive ourselves, and the truth is not in us. If we confess our sins, he is faithful and just to forgive us our sins, and to cleanse us from all unrighteousness. If we say that we have not sinned, we make him a liar, and his word is not in us. (1 John 1)

Chapter 4

Staying Connected to God

The foundation of America is based on the belief in God and on freedom of religion. The forefathers of America started this country trusting God, and we as a nation should continue trusting God. Likewise, Christians, started with Jesus Christ, accepting Him as Lord and Savior, and should also continue with Him. Once we are born again, we are connected to the body of Christ. After salvation, it is up to us to stay connected to God and grow in Him. Maturing and growing in Christ is accomplished as we read God's Word, pray, and live our lives according to the will of God to the best of our ability.

In the beginning, as new converts, we were on fire for the Lord – we told everyone we met about Christ Jesus. Where has our enthusiasm gone? Why have we left our first love? Many Christians leave their churches for various reasons: some become bored, dissatisfied, deceived by the enemy, or even offended with another saint. Some may have valid reasons for leaving while others may not, but for whatever reason they go unchurch and disconnected from God and other believers. They are out there, on their own, uncovered, failing in life, and can't figure out why. It is God and His many blessing that makes us successful and strong. "For it is in him we live, move, and have our being" (Acts17:28).

When we sin, make mistakes, fail, or fall, we should repent, pick ourselves up, dust ourselves off, move on, and try again. We can repent as often as needed during our Christian walk. We should not let our failures disconnect us from God. God forgives us our sin and remembers them no more. If God can forget what we have done, then we should be able to do the same (Isaiah 43:25). We should not let the mistakes of our past hinder us from the promises of God. The Word tells us there is only one unforgivable sin and that is blasphemy against the Holy Spirit (Mark 3:28-29). We should stay connected to God and with other saints because the Bible tells us not to forsake the assembling of ourselves together with other believers and that iron sharpens iron – there is strength in numbers (Hebrews 10:25; Proverbs 27:17). The Bible tells us that one can chase a thousand and two can put ten thousand to flight (Deuteronomy 32:30). The Word tell us that a cord of three is not easily broken (Ecclesiastes 4:12). It is the Word of God that lets us know that there are more for us than who are against us, and if God be for us, who can be against us? (2 Kings 6:16; Romans 8:31). In our efforts to stay connected to God, we should spend time alone with God. We should be thanking Him, praising Him, and worshipping Him because He is a good God and worthy of all praise, honor, and glory. God is our power source, and without Him we can do nothing; we are powerless and are doomed for failure. Without God, we can do nothing, but with God all things are possible (Matthew 19:26). In the book of John, chapter 15, it says that Jesus Christ is the true vine, and if we do not stay connected to Him, we will wither and die. Stay with God and live! Staying connected to God provides peace, protection, favor, strength, and power. God's provisions are endless because God has everything we need. When we are connected to God, we should be obedient to the leading of the Holy Spirit, who is our Comforter, our teacher, our leader, and our guide. When we stay connected to Jesus, we will prosper and grow, but on our own we will not succeed. Living our lives disconnected from God, sets us up for failure, discontentment, and death. So, if this is you, then it is time to reconnect with God. Let go of any past hurt, pain, or resentment, because time is of an essence, life is short, and tomorrow is not promised. Return back to Jesus while you can. Turn back to God and continue with Him. When we draw near unto God, He will draw near unto us (James 4:8). We should seek the Lord while He may be found (Isaiah 55:6).

According to the Bible, when we seek God early, we will find Him (Proverbs 8:17). King David said, I was glad when they said unto me let us go in to the house of the Lord (Psalm 122:1). We should let the habitation of the Lord be our hiding place and abide there, because when we abide with God there is divine protection, provision, safety, and favor (Psalm 91:1-12, 27: 5). When we stay connected to God and His Word abides in us, we are protected from the traps and snares of Satan (1 John 2:14). Stay connected to God and live. We should continue to put God first in our lives and try to do our very best to live according to His will. We are to honor God, thank Him, and bless His holy name. We know that God is worthy. He is the source of all the good things in our lives. The Word says that "every good gift and every perfect gift is from above, and cometh down from the Father of lights, with whom is no variableness, neither shadow of turning" (James 1:17). "I have been young, and now am old; yet have I not seen the righteous forsaken, nor his seed begging bread" (Psalm 37:25).

We must stay on fire for God and not become complacent or lukewarm because God's Word says that He will spew us out of His mouth if we allow ourselves to fall into this condition (Revelation 3:16). It is vital that we put God first in our lives and have a reverence for God and the things of God. We must stay connected to Him through His Word, prayer, praise, and worship. We should spend quality time with God everyday. John 15:7 says that "if ye abide in me, and my words abide in you, ye shall ask what ye will, and it shall be done unto you." With God, all things are possible but on our own we can do nothing (Mark 10:27; John 15:5). If we don't stay connected to Jesus Christ we will die (John 15:6). Jesus said, "I am the vine, and my Father is the husbandmen" (John 15:1). Life is in the vine (John 15:1-6). We are to stay connected to Jesus Christ. Abide in Christ and live!

Seven Steps to Stay Connected to God

- **Stay in the Word:** 2 Timothy 2:15; Joshua 1:8
- **Continue in prayer:** 1 Thessalonians 5:17; Matthew 6:5-15; 2 Chronicles 7:14; Philippians 4:6

- **Keep your heart clean:** Psalm 51
- **Keep your mind and thoughts right:** Romans 8:1, 8:12:2; 2 Corinthians 10:4-5; Philippians 3:13-15
- **Keep your actions and motive pure:** Matthew 6: 33; Proverbs 3:5-10
- **Forgive:** Matthew 6:12, 14, 15
- **Finally, love God, love yourself, and love others:**

Jesus answered, "The first of all the commandments is, Hear O Israel; The Lord our God is one Lord: And thou shalt love the Lord thy God with all thy heart, and with all thy soul, and with all thy mind, and with all thy strength: this is the first commandment.

And the second is like, namely this, Thou shall love thy neighbour as thyself. There is none other commandment greater than these. (Mark 12:29-31)

Staying Connected to God through Scripture

I AM the true vine, and my Father is the husbandman. Every branch in me that beareth not fruit he taketh away: and every branch that beareth fruit, he purgeth it, that it may bring forth more fruit. Now ye are clean through the word which I have spoke unto you. Abide in me, and I in you. As the branch cannot bear fruit of itself, except it abide in the vine; no more can ye, except ye abide in me. I am the vine, ye are the branches; He that abideth in me, and I in him, the same bringeth forth much fruit: for without me ye can do nothing. If a man abide not in me, he is cast forth as a branch, and is withered; and men gather them, and cast them into the fire, and they are burned. If ye abide in me, and my words abide in you, ye shall ask what ye will, and it shall be done unto you. Herein is my Father glorified, that ye bear much fruit; so shall ye be my disciples. As the Father hath loved me, so have I loved you: continue ye in my love. If ye keep my commandments, ye shall abide in my love; even as I have kept my Father's commandments, and abide in his love. These things have I spoken unto you, that my joy might remain in you, and that your joy might be full. This is my commandment, That ye love one another, as I have loved you. Greater love hath no man than this, that a man lay down his life for his friends. Ye are my friends, if ye do whatsoever I command you. Henceforth I call you not servants; for the servant knoweth not what his lord doeth: but I have called you friends; for all things that I have heard of my Father I have made known unto you. Ye have not chosen me, but I have chosen you, and ordained you, that ye should go and bring forth fruit, and that your fruit should remain: that whatsoever ye shall ask of the Father in my name, he may give it you. These things I command you, that ye love one another. If the world hate you, ye know that it hated me before it hated you. If ye were of the world, the world would love his own; but because ye are not of the world, but I have chosen you out of the world, therefore the world hateth you. Remember the word that I said unto you, The servant is not greater than his lord. If they have persecuted me, they will also persecute you; if they have kept my saying, they will keep yours also. But all these things will they do unto you for my name's sake, because they know not him that sent me. If I had not come and spoke unto them, they had not had sin: but now they have no cloke for their sin. He that hateth me hateth my Father also. If I had not done among them the works which none other man did, they had not sin: but now have they both seen and hated both me and my Father. But this cometh to pass, that the word might be fulfilled that is written in the law, They hated me without a cause. But when the Comforter is come, whom I will send unto you from the Father, even the Spirit of truth, which proceedeth from the Father, he shall testify of me. And ye also shall bear witness, because ye have been with me from the beginning. (John 15)

***

Fret not thyself because of evildoers, neither be thou envious against the workers of iniquity.

For they shall soon be cut down like the grass, and wither as the green herb. Trust in the Lord, and do good; so shalt thou dwell in the land, and verily thou shalt be fed. Delight thyself also in the Lord; and he shall give thee the desires of thine heart. Commit thy way unto the Lord; trust also in him; and he shall bring it to pass. And he shall bring forth thy righteousness as the light, and thy judgement as the noonday. Rest in the Lord, and wait patiently for him: fret not thyself because of him who prospereth in his way, because of the man who bringeth wicked devices to pass. Cease from anger, and forsake wrath: fret not thyself in any wise to do evil. For evildoers shall be cut off: but those that wait upon the Lord, they shall inherit the earth. For yet a little while, and the wicked shall not be: yea, thou shalt diligently consider his place, and it shall not be. But the meek shall inherit the earth; and shall delight themselves in the abundance of peace. The wicked plotteth against the just, and gnasheth upon him with his teeth. The Lord shall laugh at him; for he seeth that his day is coming. The wicked have drawn out the sword, and have bent their bow, to cast down the poor and needy, and to slay such as be of upright conversation. Their sword shall enter into their own heart, and their bows shall be broken. A little that a righteous man hath is better than the riches of many wicked. For the arms of the wicked shall be broken: but the Lord upholdeth the righteous. The Lord knoweth the days of the upright: and their inheritance shall be for ever. They shall not be ashamed in the evil time: and in the days of famine they shall be satisfied. But the wicked shall perish, and the enemies of the Lord shall be as the fat of lambs: they shall consume; into smoke shall they consume away. The wicked borroweth, and payeth not again: but the righteous sheweth mercy, and giveth. For such as be blessed of him shall inherit the earth; and they that be cursed of him shall be cut off. The steps of a good man are ordered by the Lord: and he delighteth in his way. Though he fall, he shall not be utterly cast down: for the Lord upholdeth him with his hand. I have been young, and now am old; yet I have not seen the righteous forsaken, nor his seed begin bread. He is ever merciful, and lendeth; and his seed is blessed. Depart from evil, and do good; and dwell for evermore.

For the Lord loveth judgement, and forsaketh not his saints; they are preserved for ever: but the seed of the wicked shall be cut off. The righteous shall inherit the land, and dwell therein for ever. The mouth of the righteous speaketh wisdom, and his tongue talketh of judgment. The law of his God is in his heart; none of his steps shall slide. The wicked watched the righteous, and seeketh to slay him. The Lord will not leave him in his hand, nor condemn him when he is judged. Wait on the Lord, and keep his way, and he shall exalt thee to inherit the land: when the wicked are cut off, thou shalt see it. I have seen the wicked in great power, and spreading himself like a green bay tree. Yet he passed away, and, lo, he was not: yea, I sought him, but he could not be found. Mark the perfect man, and behold the upright: for the end of that man is peace. But the transgressors shall be destroyed together: the end of the wicked shall be cut off.

But the salvation of the righteous is of the Lord: he is their strength in the time of trouble.

And the Lord shall help them, and deliver them: he shall deliver them from the wicked, and save them, because they trust in him. (Psalm 37)

Conclusion

"In God We Trust" is a declarative statement that is made to show one's intent. In the beginning, America's founding fathers proclaimed their trust in God. We too are to trust God. This nation started with God and should continue with God. Christians also started with God and should continue with God. We must stand up for what we believe. I am standing up for what I believe to be true. We can depend on God because it is only God who can help us when we are in trouble. We are living in troublesome times, a time when we don't know what may happen from one moment to the next or what we may have to face on today or tomorrow, but what we do know is this; with God on our side, we will always be victorious, and everything will work out for our good (1 Corinthians 15:57). With so much uncertainty in the world, we can put our trust in this one sure thing, we can trust in a God who does not change. God is the same today, tomorrow, even forevermore (Hebrews 13:8). God loves us and wants us free from sin and death. He gave His Son, so that we might live. God's gift of salvation is free. This gift of God is available to everyone, if only you believe. After we are born again, we can grow in

Christ and get closer to Him. As we grow, our faith will increase, and we will learn to trust God more and more.

If you have found yourself in a backslidden condition, you can always repent and return to God. We can repent and return to God at any time because God loves the whole world and doesn't want anyone to be lost. God always warns His people before destruction (Genesis 6:5-15, 18:17-33). Therefore, it will benefit us if we take a closer look at what is going on with us and in the world today. Please open your heart and mind to the message in this book because judgment is at hand! God is God and He is real! Heaven and hell are real! Don't be deceived and believe there isn't a God. Don't be deceived and believe that we won't have to give an account for our lives. It does matter what we do, think, and say. Galatians 6:7-8 says, "Be not deceived; God is not mocked; for whatsoever a man soweth, that shall he also reap. For he that soweth to his flesh shall of the flesh reap corruption; but he that soweth to the Spirit shall of the Spirit reap life everlasting."

Jesus Christ is the Son of God and eternal life is available through Him. We should come to Jesus today while we can – don't wait for tomorrow. Come to Jesus today before it is too late. We should come to Jesus Christ while the blood is still running warm in our veins. If you don't know Jesus Christ as your Lord and Savior, then get to know Him! Romans 14:10-12 tells us that one day we will all stand before the judgment seat of Christ and every knee shall bow and every tongue shall confess to God. Everyone will give an account of themselves to God. We can do it now or later! Isaiah 40:10 says "Behold, the Lord God will come with strong hand, and his arm shall rule for him: behold, his reward is with him, and his work before him." It is my prayer that the Lord help us to see our true condition before it is too late.

If you are saved, stay in faith and don't compromise on your belief. Be willing to take a stand for what is right, no matter what the consequences. We don't have to worry because God will fight our battles, and He will keep us in perfect peace when our minds are stayed on Him (2 Chronicles 20:15; Philippians 4:6-8; Isaiah 26:3). We should not be weary in well doing, but stay focused, and continue with God. He will reward us in the end if we faint not (Galatians 6:9). Psalm 24:3-4 says, "Who shall ascend into the hill of the Lord? Or who shall stand in his holy place? He that hath clean hands, and a pure heart; who hath not lifted up his soul unto vanity, nor sworn deceitfully." Proverbs 16:6 says, "by mercy and truth iniquity is purged: and by fear of the Lord men depart from evil." God is still speaking today, and we should listen. We are to trust God and be willing to rely on Him because He never changes and is found faithful (Proverbs 16:6; Deuteronomy 7:9). Psalm 33:12 says, blessed is the nation whose God is the Lord. By the blessing of the upright the city is exalted: but it is overthrown by the mouth of the wicked (Proverbs 11:11). "For the nation and kingdom that will not serve thee shall perish; yea those nations shall be utterly wasted" (Isaiah 60:12). "But let all those that put their trust in thee rejoice: let them ever shout for joy, because thou defendest them: let them also that love thy name be joyful in thee for thou, Lord wilt bless the righteous; with favour wilt thou compass him as with a shield"

(Psalm 5: 11-12). We will find everything we need, when we are connected to the almighty God. It is better to trust in the Lord than to put confidence in man (Psalm 118:8).

"I will say of the Lord, He is my refuge and my fortress: my God; in him will I trust." – Psalm 91:2

A Word from the Author

I am sounding the alarm! The Day of Judgment is coming and it doesn't matter whether you believe it or not; it doesn't make it less true.

To the church: Please read the first three chapters of Revelation, and he that has an ear let him hear. Proverbs 2:6 says, "For the Lord giveth wisdom: out of His mouth cometh knowledge and understanding."

To America: The United States of America was founded on God. God was the solid foundation on which this nation stands, and without God we are sure to fail.

"Blessed is the nation whose God is the Lord" (Psalm 33:12).

"Righteous exalteth a nation: but sin is a reproach to any people" (Proverbs 14:34).

"The eyes of the Lord are in every place, beholding the evil and the good" (Proverbs 15:3).

To the people: No man is an island; that he lives and die unto himself. For in God "we live, and move, and have our being" (Acts 17:28). There is a righteous God whose eyes are everywhere and sees the good and evil. One day we will all have to give an account for every idle word and deed (Proverbs 15:3; Matthew 12:36).

The decisions we make today will determine our tomorrows:

- "Trust in the Lord with all thine heart; and to lean not unto thine own understanding. In all thy ways acknowledge him, and He shall direct thy path" (Proverbs 3:5-6).
- "There is a way which seemeth right unto a man, but the end thereof are the ways of death" (Proverbs 14:12).
- "And even as they did not like to retain God in their knowledge, God gave them over to a reprobate mind, to do those things which are not convenient" (Romans 1:28).

"I have set before you, life and death, blessing and cursing: therefore choose life, that both thou and thy seed may live" - Deuteronomy 30:19

I encourage you today to choose Jesus Christ and live.

"They will be my people and I will be their God." - Jeremiah 32:38

Plan of Salvation

According to Romans 10:9-10, "If thou shalt confess with thy mouth the Lord Jesus, and shalt believe in thine hearts that God hath raised him from the dead, thou shalt be saved. For with the heart man believeth unto righteousness; and with the mouth confession is made unto salvation."

Ephesians 2:8 tells us that "by grace are ye saved through faith; and that not of yourselves: it is the gift of God: Not of works, lest any man should boast. For we are his workmanship, created in Christ Jesus unto good works, which God hath before ordained that we should walk in them."

Jesus said in John 10:10 that "the thief cometh not, but for to steal, and to kill, and to destroy: I am come that they might have life, and that they might have it more abundantly."

> "Jesus saith unto him, I am the way, the truth and the life: no man cometh unto the Father but by me" (John 14:6).

The Bible tells us that if we confess our sins, He is

faithful and just to forgive us our sins, and to cleanse us from all unrighteousness (1 John 1:9).

> "Then he called for a light and sprang in, and came trembling, and fell down before Paul and Silas, And brought them out and said, Sirs, what must I do to be saved? And they said, Believe on the Lord Jesus Christ, and thou shalt be saved, and thy house. And they spake unto him the word of the Lord, and to all that were in his house" (Acts 16:29-32).

The Bible tells us in John 3:14-18 "As Moses lifted up the serpent in the wilderness, even so must the Son of man be lifted up: That whosoever believeth in him should not perish, but have eternal life. For God so loved the world, that he gave his only begotten Son, that whosoever believeth in him should not perish but have everlasting life. For God sent not his Son into the world to condemn the world; but that the world through him might be saved. He that believeth on him is not condemned: but he that believeth not is condemned already, because he hath not believed in the name of the only begotten Son of God."

In John 3:3, Jesus tells Nicodemus, "Verily, verily, I say unto thee, Except a man be born again, he cannot see the Kingdom of God."

Notes

Notes

About the Author

B. B. Hicks is author of two previous books, *7 Daily Confessions*, and *Overcoming Hurt God's Way*. She is native of Lamont, Mississippi, and she is the daughter of the late evangelist Florence Maiten. She is a wife, mother, and grandmother. She was baptized at age six and rededicated her life to Christ in June 2004. B. B. Hicks is saved, loves the Lord, and is a woman who studies and teaches the Word of God.

Notes

Printed in the United States
By Bookmasters